OUR GOVERNMENT

Congress
and the Legislative Branch

Bryon Giddens-White

Heinemann
LIBRARY

Chicago, Illinois

Designed by David Poole and Calcium
Illustrations by Geoff Ward
Originated by P.T. Repro Multi Warna
Printed in China by WKT Company Limited

07 06 05
10 9 8 7 6 5 4 3 2 1

Library of Congress Cataloging-in-Publication Data
Giddens-White, Bryon.
  Congress and the legislative branch / Bryon Giddens-White.
      p. cm. -- (Our government)
  Includes bibliographical references and index.
  ISBN 1-4034-6602-5 (hc) -- ISBN 1-4034-6607-6 (pb)
  1. United States. Congress--Juvenile literature. I. Title: Congress and the legislative branch. II. Title. III. Series.
  JK1025.G53 2006
  328.73--dc22
                                    2005008665

Acknowledgments
AP Wide World Photo pp. 10 (John Duricka), 13 (Ed Andrieski), 17, 18 (Dennis Cook), 22 (Ron Edmonds); Corbis pp. 6 (Bettmann), 8 (Bettmann), 14 (Wally McNamee), 21 (Brooks Kraft), 26 (Philip Gould), 27 (Reuters/Larry Downing), 29 (Francis G. Mayer); Getty Images pp. 1 (Stone/Doug Armand), 25 (William Thomas Cain), 28 (PhotoDisc/Hisham F. Ibrahim); Library of Congress pp. 5, 12; National Archive and Records Administration p. 7; North Wind Picture Archives p. 9; One Mile Up, Inc. p. 16.

Cover photograph of the Capital Building, Washington D.C. reproduced with permission of Getty Images (Stone/Doug Armand.)

Every effort has been made to contact copyright holders of any material reproduced in this book. Any omissions will be rectified in subsequent printings if notice is given to the publishers.

Special thanks to Gary Barr and Paula McClain for their help in the production of this book.

Contents

Bleeding Kansas 4

Introduction to the Legislative Branch 6

The Great Compromise 8

The House of Representatives 10

The Senate 12

Legislative Checks and Balances 14

The Powers and Duties of Congress 16

Leaders and Committees in Congress 18

How Congress Makes Laws 20

Landmark Legislation of Congress 22

Interest Groups and Lobbyists 24

A Day in the Life of a Member
of Congress 26

All About the Capitol 28

Glossary 30

Further Reading 31

Index 32

Any words appearing in the text in bold, **like this**, are explained in the Glossary.

Bleeding Kansas

To many people, the United States is a symbol of freedom. People can practice any religion they want, or choose not to practice a religion. They can express their ideas in public, even if they criticize the government. And they are guaranteed the right to pursue their own happiness. But in the beginning of United States history, not everyone was granted these rights.

Slavery was first practiced in the United States in the 1600s, when the first colonies were formed. During the American Revolution (1775–1783), when the thirteen original colonies fought for freedom from Great Britain, many slaves hoped that they would gain freedom, too. It was not to be. In fact, after the colonies won their independence, slavery was written into the **Constitution** and protected by law.

In the 1800s, the **abolitionist** movement gained strength, especially in the northern states. At the same time, plantation owners in the South were getting rich selling cotton and other crops that were picked by thousands and thousands of slaves. Slave owners did not want slavery to end.

The clash between abolitionists in the North and slave owners in the South became increasingly heated as the mid-1800s approached. **Representatives** from both sides debated slavery in the **legislative branch**, the part of the government that makes laws. In the 1850s, the debate got ugly.

At this time, the United States was growing as a nation and adding new territories. **Congress** (the legislative body of the U.S. government) had to decide whether the people in these territories could have slaves. Representatives in Congress who supported abolition did not want slavery to exist in the new territories. Pro-slavery representatives wanted the new territories to have slaves.

In 1854, Congress had to **resolve** the slavery issue for two new territories that would come to be known as Kansas and Nebraska.

A member of Congress named Stephen A. Douglas **sponsored** a law that would allow people living in the new territories to vote whether to become a slave state or free state. With the support of the president, the law was passed.

Since Nebraska was so far north, it was certain to vote against slavery. But it was unclear how Kansas would vote. Before the election took place, hundreds of northern abolitionists quickly moved to Kansas to try to influence the vote in their favor. They carried weapons, determined to keep the territory free from slavery. When people from the South arrived, they had weapons, too. Violence erupted throughout Kansas, particularly after the vote on slavery was held in 1855 and the pro-slavery side won. For years, buildings in Kansas were burned and people were murdered. The period from 1854–1859 came to be known as "Bleeding Kansas."

During this period in United States history, the legislative branch played a crucial role in shaping the direction of the country. Shortly after the Civil War (1861–1865) came to an end, Congress **ratified** the Thirteenth Amendment of the Constitution, which outlawed slavery.

▲ The 1854 Kansas-Nebraska Act led to brutal events such as the "Sack of Lawrence." Kansas was the scene of so much violence that it earned the nickname "Bleeding Kansas."

Introduction to the Legislative Branch

Fact File

Number of Houses: Two

Names of Houses: The House of Representatives and the Senate

Location: U.S. Capitol, Washington, D.C.

Number of Members: House of Representatives: 435 Senate: 100

Term of Office: Representative: Two years Senator: Six years

Minimum Age: Representative: 25 Senator: 30

Presiding Officers: House of Representatives: Speaker of the House; Senate: the Vice President of the United States

Main Duty: Make **federal** (national) laws

During the spring of 1787, a group of men gathered to make a plan for the government of the United States. The written document that they created is called a constitution. Constitutions describe the powers and duties of a country's government. They also contain important laws, such as those that protect the rights of the country's citizens.

The U.S. Constitution divided the government into three branches, or parts. The three branches are the legislative branch, the **executive branch**, and the **judicial branch**. The legislative branch makes the laws. The executive branch carries out and **enforces** the laws. The judicial branch interprets (tells the meaning of) the laws and makes sure that they agree with the Constitution.

The framers of the Constitution believed that the legislative branch was the most important branch of the government. This is the reason it appears first in the Constitution. The legislative branch has an

enormous influence over the social and economic life of the United States. The authors of the Constitution were aware of its power and worked hard to design a legislative branch that would be acceptable to the state governments. In the next section, you will read about the plan they created.

◄ Prior to the U.S. Constitution, states operated under the Articles of Confederation (1781-89). Although this document gave limited powers to the national government, it paved the way for the U.S. Constitution.

◄ Men from all over the United States traveled to Philadelphia in 1787. They made a plan for the U.S. government that we still use today—the Constitution.

7

The Great Compromise

When the nation's founders gathered in 1787 to write the Constitution, the United States had just thirteen states. Every state except Rhode Island sent **delegates** to help write the Constitution. These delegates had different ideas about what sort of government the United States should have. Over the course of the summer, they exchanged ideas and worked through disagreements until they came up with a plan that satisfied as many delegates as possible.

Everyone agreed that one part of the United States government should be in charge of making laws. As you have read, this is the duty of the legislative branch, which is also known as Congress. The delegates also agreed that each state would vote for its own representatives to send to Congress. These representatives would meet to make laws for the entire nation. However, the delegates disagreed about how many representatives each state should have.

◄ The New Jersey Plan was also known as the Paterson Plan, named after one of its authors, William Paterson.

States with larger populations thought they should have more representatives in the legislative branch. They favored the Virginia Plan, which called for representation according to the size of a state's population. But states with smaller populations did not think this was a fair plan. They favored the New Jersey Plan, which called for the same number of representatives from each state.

The delegates from both sides realized that they would need to settle for less than what they originally wanted. They finally worked out a plan, called the **Great Compromise**, which divided the legislative branch into two houses, or parts. One house was to be called the **Senate**. The other would be called the **House of Representatives**.

Each state legislature would appoint two representatives to the Senate. This answered the concerns of the smaller states because every state had equal power within one branch of Congress. However, representation in the House of Representatives would be based on the population of the states. This satisfied the wishes of the larger states, which wanted a larger number of representatives.

Neither side was entirely happy with the Great Compromise, but on July 16, 1787, it was passed by one vote. In the following sections, you will read more about how the delegates organized the two houses of the legislative branch.

▲ The Great Compromise was also called the Connecticut Compromise because it was proposed by a delegate from Connecticut named Roger Sherman.

The House of Representatives

The House of Representatives is sometimes called the "people's house." This is for two reasons. Members of the House of Representatives, called **congressmen** or representatives, often have a closer relationship with the people they serve than senators because they represent smaller populations and smaller areas. Secondly, representatives have always been elected by **popular vote** and have shorter terms than senators. This allows voters to show dislike or support for their representatives fairly frequently through elections.

Each House member represents a part of his or her state, called a **congressional district**. States with larger populations are divided into several congressional districts. Some states with smaller populations form a single congressional district.

▼ In this photograph, members of the House of Representatives take the oath of office.

Distribution of the House of Representatives by State

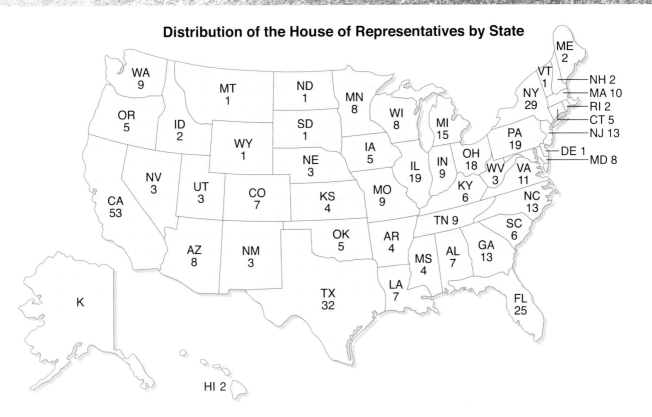

The very first House of Representatives had 65 members, one for every 30,000 people. As the country grew in population, more and more members were added. Each state has at least one representative. In 1929, Congress passed a law that limited the number of House members to 435.

As a state's population grows or declines, its number of representatives can change. Every ten years, the U.S. Census Bureau counts the total U.S. population and makes adjustments to the number of representatives each state has. Some states lose representatives and some states gain them, but the total number of representatives in the House remains 435.

There are several requirements that must be met in order to become a representative. **Candidates** for the House have to be at least 25 years old and must have been a citizen of the United States for at least seven years. In addition, candidates must live in the state they wish to represent.

In the next section, you will learn about the founders' plan for the other house of the legislative branch, the Senate.

▲ This map shows the allocation of representatives to the House of Representatives through 2010.

The Senate

While the House of Representatives was created to voice the interests of the people, the Senate was formed to focus on the broader interests of the country. The authors of the Constitution purposefully organized the two branches to promote these different interests.

First, they created a different election process for senators. Citizens have always directly elected members of the House of Representatives. However, at the beginning of our nation's history, the people elected senators indirectly. They first elected members of their state legislative branches. Then their state representatives elected their senators.

In 1870, Hiram Revels ▶ of Mississippi became the first African American to be elected to the Senate by his state legislature.

This process served two purposes. On the one hand, it gave specific powers to the state governments. This was important to the founders, who wanted to divide power between the national and state governments. They also hoped this process would result in the election of more qualified and capable people.

This indirect system of voting for senators survived until 1913. In that year, Congress passed the Seventeenth Amendment, which provided for the direct election of Senators by popular vote.

The founders also sought other means for establishing wisdom and stability in the Senate. Like House members, senators must live in the state they intend to represent. However, the Constitution requires senators to be 5 years older than House members—at least 30 years old—and to have been a citizen of the United States for 9 rather than 7 years.

Senators serve six-year **terms**—three times the term length for House members. The founders believed that longer terms were necessary for senators to become familiar with the affairs and laws of the nation.

▼ Politics often runs in the family. U.S. Senator Ken Salazar (center, right) and his brother, U.S. Representative John Salazar (center, left), were both elected to office in Colorado in 2004.

Legislative Checks and Balances

The authors of the Constitution wanted to make sure that the national government did not have too much power. They decided to give certain powers to the national government and other powers to the state governments. This is called a **federal system**. Then they divided the national government into three branches, creating a **separation of powers**. Finally, they created a system in which each branch could check, or limit, the powers of the other branches. In this way, a balance of power would exist among the three branches. This is called a system of **checks and balances**.

Legislative and Executive Checks

The legislative branch has an important check on the executive branch through the Senate's power to reject treaties and nominations made by the president. The legislative branch also has the power to remove a president from office if it **impeaches** and convicts a president of "treason, bribery, or other high crimes and misdemeanors."

In 1998, the House of ▶ Representatives voted to impeach President William Clinton, accusing the president of committing perjury and obstruction of justice. However, the Senate voted that Clinton was not guilty of the impeachment charges.

Legislative Checks and Balances

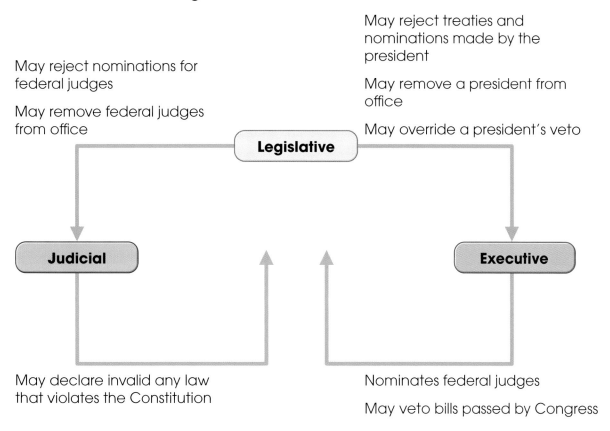

May reject nominations for federal judges

May remove federal judges from office

May reject treaties and nominations made by the president

May remove a president from office

May override a president's veto

Legislative

Judicial

Executive

May declare invalid any law that violates the Constitution

Nominates federal judges

May veto bills passed by Congress

One of the most powerful checks the Constitution gives to the executive branch is the presidential veto. The president can either sign or veto (reject) legislative **bills**. If the president vetoes a bill, it cannot become a law unless two-thirds of the members of both houses of Congress vote to **override** the veto.

Legislative and Judicial Checks

The legislative branch also has checks on the judicial branch. Although the president has the power to nominate federal judges, including Supreme Court **justices**, the Senate can vote to reject the president's nominees. The legislative branch also has the power to remove federal judges who commit "treason, bribery, or other high crimes and misdemeanors."

One of the judicial branch's most powerful checks was added after the Constitution was written. **Judicial review** is the power of the Supreme Court to decide whether the laws created by the legislative branch agree with the Constitution. The Supreme Court has the power to declare invalid any law that violates the Constitution.

The Powers and Duties of Congress

As you know, the main function of the legislative branch is to legislate, or make laws. The Constitution gives Congress lawmaking powers in many areas. For example, Congress has the power to:

- create new money
- levy (impose and collect) taxes
- award patents and copyrights
- make citizenship rules
- create lower federal courts
- establish post offices and roads
- raise armed forces and declare war
- admit new states to the Union
- propose amendments to the Constitution

The authors of the Constitution knew that they would not be able to predict all of the powers that Congress would need. Therefore, they included the "necessary and proper" clause. This clause states that Congress has the authority and flexibility to expand its power to deal with new situations the founders never imagined.

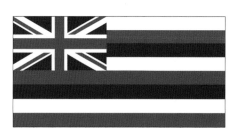

The last states ▶ that Congress admitted into the Union were Alaska and Hawaii in 1959. Pictured to the right are the flags of Alaska (top) and Hawaii (bottom).

In addition to describing the general duties and powers of Congress, the Constitution also assigns certain powers to each house. For example, the Constitution gives the "power of the purse" to the House of Representatives. This means that all legislation related to taxes or raising **revenue** must begin in the House. In addition, the House alone has the authority to accuse government officials of wrongdoing in a process called impeachment.

Although the House has the authority to impeach officials, the Senate holds the trial to determine whether the official is guilty of the charges. If the Senate **convicts** the official, he or she is then removed from office.

The Constitution also gives the Senate the power to approve or reject many of the nominations made by the president, including nominations of Supreme Court justices and ambassadors. Finally, the Senate has the authority to approve or reject treaties with other countries that are made by the president.

▼ On December 7, 1941, Japan attacked the American naval base at Pearl Harbor in Hawaii. President Roosevelt called it "a date which will live in infamy" and asked Congress to declare war on Japan. Shortly afterward, Congress voted, with one dissent, for a declaration of war.

Leaders and Committees in Congress

Political parties have a major influence on leadership in Congress. The party with the most members in a house of Congress is called the **majority party**. The party with fewer members is called the **minority party**. The leaders of each house of Congress are usually determined by the majority party.

In most cases, the House of Representatives chooses a member of the majority party to become the House leader, called the **Speaker of the House**. The speaker has a great deal of influence over which legislation gets the attention of House members.

According to the Constitution, the vice president of the United States is the leader of the Senate. However, since the vice president only participates in the Senate on special occasions, the member of the majority party who has been there the longest usually becomes the Senate leader when the vice president is absent.

▼ Representative Nancy Pelosi (below) of California is the current House minority leader in Congress. She is the first woman to lead either house of Congress.

Leaders of Congress

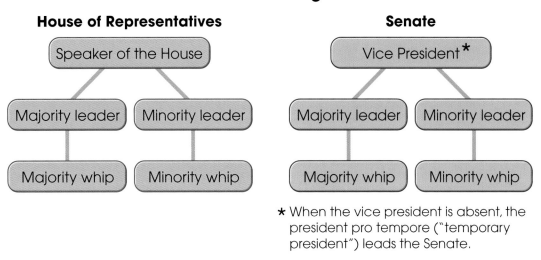

House of Representatives

- Speaker of the House
  - Majority leader
    - Majority whip
  - Minority leader
    - Minority whip

Senate

- Vice President*
  - Majority leader
    - Majority whip
  - Minority leader
    - Minority whip

★ When the vice president is absent, the president pro tempore ("temporary president") leads the Senate.

Over time, other leadership positions have developed. In each house of Congress, the party with the most members elects a majority leader, and the party with fewer members elects a minority leader. These "floor leaders" exercise a lot of influence over legislative business. Parties also elect majority and minority whips, who work with floor leaders to "whip up" support among members for legislation favored by their party.

Parties also have great influence over **committee** appointments. Committees are subgroups created by each branch of Congress to divide up its lawmaking duties. Each committee specializes in a certain area of the law, such as foreign affairs, banking, agriculture, or commerce. The House of Representatives currently has nineteen standing, or permanent, committees. The Senate has sixteen. In the next section, you will learn about the role of committees in the lawmaking process.

How Congress Makes Laws

Congress creates laws that touch every aspect of life in our country, such as ensuring that we have clean air and water and that all people are treated equally.

Anyone can create an idea for a law. The president, members of Congress, individuals, groups of citizens, or even children can propose a law. However, only a senator or a member of the House of Representatives can sponsor a bill—an early version of a new law—in Congress. Once a representative sponsors a bill, it must go through a number of different steps before it can become a law. These steps, described below, are similar in both houses of Congress.

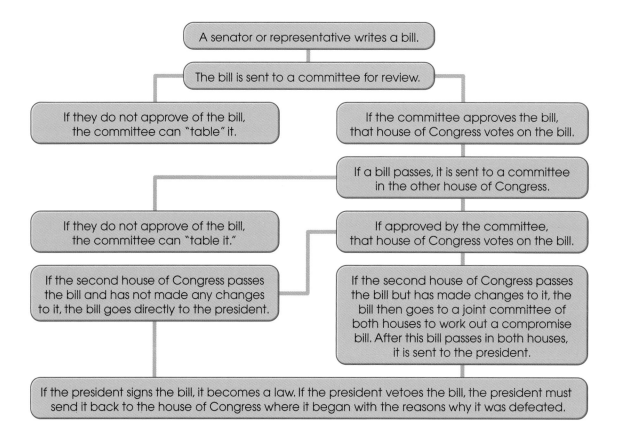

A senator or representative writes a bill.

The bill is sent to a committee for review.

If they do not approve of the bill, the committee can "table" it.

If the committee approves the bill, that house of Congress votes on the bill.

If a bill passes, it is sent to a committee in the other house of Congress.

If they do not approve of the bill, the committee can "table it."

If approved by the committee, that house of Congress votes on the bill.

If the second house of Congress passes the bill and has not made any changes to it, the bill goes directly to the president.

If the second house of Congress passes the bill but has made changes to it, the bill then goes to a joint committee of both houses to work out a compromise bill. After this bill passes in both houses, it is sent to the president.

If the president signs the bill, it becomes a law. If the president vetoes the bill, the president must send it back to the house of Congress where it began with the reasons why it was defeated.

▲ In this photograph, President George W. Bush signs the Healthy Forests Restoration Act. This piece of legislation was passed to help prevent the devastating wildfires that occur annually in the West.

Let's follow a new law that begins in the Senate. A senator, after listening to the ideas and concerns of the people, writes a bill. Then the bill goes to a committee, where committee members discuss it. If they don't agree with the bill, they can "table" it, which means they reject it. If they approve of the bill, they can either make changes to the bill and send it back to the senator, or they can send it back without making changes.

After the committee accepts the bill, the entire Senate votes on it. For a bill to pass, more than half of the senators have to approve it. If the Senate approves the bill, it moves to the House of Representatives. The same steps are repeated in the House.

If the bill is passed in both the Senate and the House of Representatives, it then goes to the president of the United States. If the president signs the bill, it becomes a law. If the president vetoes the bill, it can still become a law if two-thirds of the House and two-thirds of the Senate vote to override the president's veto.

Landmark Legislation of Congress

A s you have read, Congress passes legislation that impacts nearly every aspect of life in the United States. Below are a number of important **acts** passed by Congress.

ENVIRONMENT
Clean Air Act (1970)
First enacted in 1970, the Clean Air Act was amended in 1990. Under this law, the government sets limits on how much of a pollutant can be in the air. The act ensures that all Americans have the same environmental health protections.

GOVERNMENT
Freedom of Information Act (1966)
The Freedom of Information Act gives citizens greater access to the federal government's records. A 1996 amendment requires federal agencies to create electronic reading rooms to make records more readily available to the public.

CIVIL RIGHTS
The Civil Rights Act (1964)
Enacted in the wake of a growing number of civil rights demonstrations, the Civil Rights Act was written to end discrimination based on race, color, religion, or national origin.

CRIME
Brady Handgun Violence Prevention Act (1993)
The Brady Act was named after White House Press Secretary James Brady, who was seriously injured in an assassination attempt on President Ronald Reagan. The act ordered a waiting period before the purchase of a handgun. It also established a national criminal background check system, which firearms dealers must contact before they sell firearms.

▼ The aftermath of the 1981 attempt to assassinate President Ronald Reagan led to the Brady gun laws.

WORKERS
Eight-Hour Workday (1892)

In 1892, Congress approved legislation that limited laborers and mechanics employed by the U.S. government to working for eight hours per day. The act suffered from lack of enforcement, and several decades passed before the eight-hour workday became the standard.

DEFENSE
Patriot Act (2001)

The Patriot Act was passed not long after the terrorist attacks of September 11, 2001. The act was created to deter terrorist acts in the United States and around the world. It also gives law enforcement more tools for preventing and punishing those acts.

CONSUMERS
Pure Food and Drug Act (1906)

This act requires that all foods and drugs be accurately labeled. It allows the government to punish persons involved in the adulteration, mislabeling, or poisoning of foods, drugs, medicines, and liquors.

ECONOMY
Sherman Antitrust Act (1890)

This act gave Congress the power to prosecute people or corporations found guilty of **monopolizing** or attempting to monopolize commerce.

SCIENCE/TECHNOLOGY
National Aeronautics and Space Act (1958)

This act created the National Aeronautics and Space Administration (NASA) to oversee nonmilitary activities relating to outer space. NASA develops research facilities, builds space vehicles, and hires scientists and engineers for the space program.

TRANSPORTATION
Federal Highway Act (1956)

The Federal Highway Act authorized more than $31 billion over a thirteen-year period for road building. The act resulted in the construction of a 41,000-mile system of Interstate Highways.

23

Interest Groups and Lobbyists

You have read about the different individuals and groups in Congress that conduct the business of the legislative branch. In this section, you will read about other groups that influence the legislative process.

Individuals vote for people to represent their interests in the legislature. Citizens also form groups in order to promote their interests in Congress. Almost every bill considered by the legislative branch attracts the attention of competing **interest groups**. Some interest groups encourage Congress to pass a bill, while others encourage Congress to alter or reject it.

There are many different kinds of interest groups. Some represent the interests of businesses, others represent workers, and still others are concerned with specific issues, such as the right to carry a weapon.

Political cartoons show up on all sides of the issues, often making fun of different groups in politics. In this cartoon, the man represents an interest group that has a "politician in its pocket." This phrase refers to a group or person that has a strong influence over politicians. ▶

NRA

I'VE PACKED ONE FOR YEARS...

Concealed weapons Bill OK'd

POLITICIANS

BRANCH ©1995 SAN ANTONIO EXPRESS-NEWS

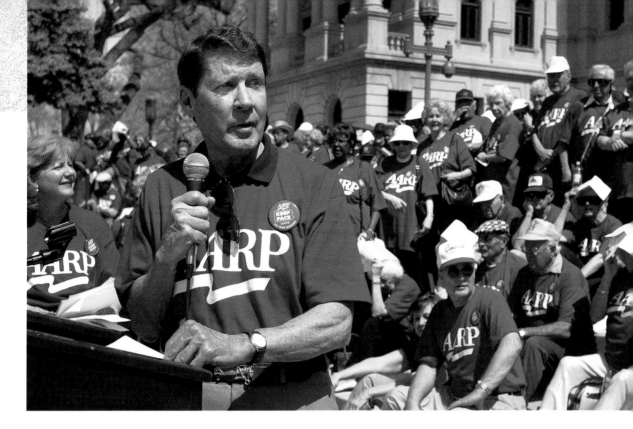

Many interest groups hire **lobbyists** to help them persuade, or lobby, lawmakers to pass laws that their group supports. Some groups have enough money to hire full-time lobbyists. Groups with less money might hire a single professional lobbyist. Successful lobbyists are educated in their field and familiar with the legislative process. They have access to the representatives and other government employees who have an influence over legislation that interests the groups for which they work.

In addition to directly lobbying public officials, lobbyists also work to win support for interest groups in indirect ways. Lobbyists initiate letter-writing campaigns, make sure that their groups' interests are positively represented by the press, and even arrange public demonstrations. Groups with lots of money tend to be more successful at lobbying.

▲ Interest groups try to influence domestic policy. In 2004, the American Association of Retired Persons worked on behalf of a bill to overhaul the Medicare system.

A Day in the Life of a Member of Congress

Almost all members of Congress have two things in common: the citizens of their congressional districts have chosen them to represent their interests in Washington, D.C., and they have all come to the capital to make laws for the United States. The daily lives of Congress members reflect these two facts.

▲ Members of Congress meet with constituents to discuss the concerns of their communities.

Morning

Most members of Congress begin work early. Newspapers and television news are usually part of the breakfast routine. Other early morning tasks might include making phone calls to staff working in the member's home state. Members of Congress pay close attention to the opinions and needs of their **constituents** (the people who they represent). After talking with staff, they will likely head to work at the **Capitol**. On the way, they might review the day's schedule or read important mail.

Midday

At the Capitol, members will likely spend some time in their office preparing for the day's events, which might include a committee meeting or a **floor debate**. If a committee meeting is scheduled, a member might review the bill under consideration. Or if the committee is to hear public **testimony**, committee members might prepare questions for **witnesses**. If a floor debate is scheduled, members are likely to focus on polishing speeches that they will deliver to express their views of the bill under consideration.

Evening

Late in the afternoon, members of Congress might arrange to speak with the press about legislative affairs. Or they might schedule a meeting with a caucus to which they belong. A caucus is a group of Congress members who join together to pursue interests common to them or their constituents. The caucus may consider upcoming bills or talk about new legislation they intend to sponsor.

After the events of late afternoon, members may return home to eat dinner and spend the evening with family. But it is also likely that dinner may be an opportunity to meet with a lobbyist or interest-group representative who wishes to discuss the member's views on upcoming bills. Members of Congress are also frequently in demand for social affairs. Evenings are often spent making public appearances or delivering speeches to organizations that are interested in the member's work.

▼ Founded in 1976, the Congressional Black Caucus Foundation (CBCF) assists today's black leaders, while helping to prepare the next generation of leaders. Below, members of the CBCF meet with President George W. Bush.

All About the Capitol

The Capitol is the name of the building in Washington, D.C., where Congress meets. It is located about a mile and a half from the **White House**.

It may surprise you to learn that Washington, D.C., was not always the nation's capital. The government first met in New York City, and then Philadelphia, before moving permanently to Washington, D.C., in 1800.

Work on the Capitol began in 1793. The Capitol's architects based their design on the architecture of Ancient Greece and Rome. Many of the political ideas that influenced the founders of the United States came from these societies. The architects wanted to show this connection in their design.

The exterior of the Capitol features a large central building and side buildings, called wings. An enormous dome of cast-iron and stone sits astride the central building. The Capitol's wings were extended in the 1850s. Many new states had joined the Union by then, and the House and Senate had outgrown their chambers, or meeting rooms.

The Capitol building has five levels. Located on the ground floor are many of the committee rooms, where representatives consider bills sponsored by members of Congress. The chambers of the House of Representatives and the Senate are located on the second floor. The

▼ The U.S. Capitol building has been through a lot since its construction first began in 1793. Today, it continues to stand as a symbol of the United States government's strength.

Rotunda is a magnificent room located on the second floor beneath the massive dome, which rises more than 180 feet above the floor.

In addition to being the meeting place of Congress, the Capitol is home to many extraordinary works of art and other artifacts from the nation's past.

Visitors to the Capitol who wish to observe Congressional proceedings go to the third floor. From there, they gain access to the galleries above the House and Senate Chambers. The rest of the third floor is occupied by more committee rooms and government offices. The fourth floor and the basement of the Capitol contain machinery rooms, workshops, and additional offices.

The work of America's legislative branch and the majesty of its home combine to make the Capitol one of the most revered buildings in the United States, and a great symbol of democracy.

▲ This painting was one of several made by John Trumbull in the early 1800s for the Capitol Rotunda. Its subject is the signing of the Declaration of Independence in Independence Hall, Philadelphia, on July 4, 1776.

Glossary

abolitionist somebody who campaigned against slavery during the eighteenth and nineteenth centuries

act name usually given to a bill that is signed into law by the president

bill early version or draft of a law

candidate someone who has qualified and is running for office

Capitol building of the legislative branch

checks and balances system that makes sure one branch of government cannot become stronger than another branch

committee subgroup created by Congress to divide the lawmaking duties of the legislative branch

Congress legislative branch of the United States; it has two houses: the Senate and the House of Representatives

congressmen can refer to senators, but is most commonly used for members of the House of Representatives

congressional district area into which states are divided for election purposes

constituent citizen who lives in the area governed or represented by someone who holds public office

constitution document containing a country's basic principles and laws; it describes the powers and duties of the government and guarantees the rights of citizens

convict declare a person guilty of a crime in a court of law

delegate representative

enforce cause obedience to a law, regulation, or command

executive branch branch of government that carries out and enforces the law

federal relating to the national government as distinct from the state governments

federal system system in which power is divided between a national and state governments

floor debate debate over a proposed bill in one of the houses of the legislative branch

Great Compromise decision reached by the authors of the Constitution that created a two-branch legislature with a Senate, in which each state was equally represented, and a House of Representatives, with representation based on population

House of Representatives lower house of the United States' legislative branch

impeach charge a public official with misconduct in public office

interest group group formed by citizens in order to advance their interests in Congress

judicial branch branch of the government that interprets the law

judicial review power held by the Supreme Court to review laws and acts of the government to make sure they agree with the Constitution

justice judge of the Supreme Court

legislative branch branch of the government that makes laws

lobbyist individual who works on behalf of a client to persuade, or lobby, lawmakers to act in the interest of his or her client

majority party political party with the largest number of members in a house of the legislative branch

minority party political party without a majority in a house of the legislative branch

monopolizing gaining exclusive control over the means of producing or selling a good or a service; monopolies usually result in unreasonably high costs for consumers

override cancel or change an action taken by somebody else

political party group of people who have similar views about government and the policies it should pursue; parties seek to influence government by getting their members elected to public office

popular vote vote of the public

ratify give formal approval of something

representative individual elected by citizens to represent them in the government

resolve come to a firm decision about something

revenue income the government collects and receives into the treasury for public use

Rotunda large room located beneath the massive dome of the Capitol

Senate upper house of the United States' legislative branch

separation of powers system of government that distributes power among several branches

Speaker of the House presiding leader in the House of Representatives

sponsor bring a bill before Congress; support

term length of time, set by law, served by an elected person

testimony declaration given by someone who is under oath, such as that given by a citizen at a committee hearing

White House official residence of the president of the United States

witness person who can give a firsthand account of an event

Further Reading

Giesecke, Ernestine. *National Government*. Chicago: Heinemann Library, 2000.

Horn, Geoffrey M. *Congress*. Circle Pines, MN: AGS Publishing, 2003.

Santella, Andrew. *The Capitol*. Chicago: Children's Press, 1995.

Index

abolitionist movement 4
age requirements 6, 11
ambassadors 17
American Association of Retired Persons 25
American Revolution 4
appointments 19

bills 15, 20
"Bleeding Kansas" 5
Brady Handgun Violence Prevention Act 22
Bush, George W. 21, 27

candidates 11
Capitol building 26, 28
caucuses 27
Census Bureau 11
chambers 28, 29
checks and balances 14, 15
Civil Rights Act 22
Civil War 5
Clean Air Act 22
Clinton, William 14
committees 19, 21, 28, 29
Congressional Black Caucus Foundation (CBCF) 27
congressional districts 10
congressmen. See representatives.
Connecticut Compromise. See Great Compromise.
constituents 26
Constitution of the United States 5, 6, 7, 8, 13, 14, 15, 16, 17, 18
Constitutional Convention 6, 8

Declaration of Independence 29
delegates 8
dome 28, 29
Douglas, Stephen A. 5

Eight Hour Workday Act 23
elections 10, 12, 13
executive branch 6, 14

Federal Highway Act 23
federal system 14
floor debates 26
"floor leaders" 19
freedom 4
Freedom of Information Act 22

Great Britain 4
Great Compromise 9
Greece 28

Healthy Forests Restoration Act 21
House Minority Leader 18
House of Representatives 6, 9, 10, 11, 12, 16, 17, 18, 19, 20, 21

impeachment 14, 17
Independence Hall, Philadelphia 29
interest groups 24, 25, 27

judicial branch 6, 15
judicial review 15
justices 15, 17

Kansas 4, 5
Kansas-Nebraska Act 5

laws 20, 21
lobbyists 25, 27

majority leader 19
majority party 18
majority whip 19
minority leader 19
minority party 18
minority whip 19

National Aeronautics and Space Act 23
Nebraska 4, 5
New Jersey Plan 9
newspapers 26
nominations 17

Paterson Plan. See New Jersey Plan.
Paterson, William 8
Patriot Act 23
Pearl Harbor, Hawaii 17
Pelosi, Nancy 18
political cartoons 13, 24
political parties 18, 19
popular vote 10, 13
"power of the purse" 16, 17
presidential veto 15, 21
presidents 5, 15, 17, 20, 21
Pure Food and Drug Act 23

ratification 5
Reagan, Ronald 22
representatives 4, 6, 8, 9, 10, 11, 18, 19, 20, 26, 27, 28
Revels, Hiram 12
revenue 17
Rome 28
Rotunda 29

"Sack of Lawrence" 5
Senate 6, 9, 12, 13, 17, 19, 21
senators 10, 13, 18, 19, 20, 21, 26, 27
separation of powers 14
Seventeenth Amendment 13
Sherman Antitrust Act 23
Sherman, Roger 9
slavery 4, 5
Speaker of the House 6, 18
state governments 13
Supreme Court 15, 17

television news 26
term of office 6, 10, 13
Thirteenth Amendment 5
treaties 17
Trumbull, John 29

veto 15, 21
vice presidents 6, 18
Virginia Plan 8, 9

Washington, D.C. 28
whips 19
White House 28
wings 28